The Book of Gratitude

Grade Two

BookLeaf Publishing

Presentation by *BookLeaf Publishing*

Web: www.bookleafpub.com

E-mail: info@bookleafpub.com

ISBN: 9789357449144

First edition 2021

The Poem of God-Couplet

Thank you God for trees.
Thank you God for bees.
Thank you God for flowers.
Thank you God for rain showers.

-Nia

Class Haiku

I love Grade 2
because it is so much fun
math and social rock.

-Levi

The Park Couplet

I love playing on the monkey bars
but I don't like the funky bars.

-Aiden

Friends Haiku

Effie, Levi, Beck.
Quinn, Miss Boddez, Hunter.
Penelope, class.

-Peyton

Playground Couplet

I play with my friends on the swings.
We laugh at so many things.

-Jaxton

Sports Haiku

I am grateful for
sports like hockey and players
like Effie, Nia, Beck.

-Beck

Nature Couplet

Thank you for the trees
and for the bees.

I am grateful for the rain,
it makes things not so plain.

-Penelope

Thank You Haiku

Thank you for my class.
Thank you for my family.
Thank you for my strength.

-Declan

Thank You Haiku

Thank you for my pet.
Thank you for my friends and school.
    Thank you for my faith.

-Luke and Ethan

Friends Poem

I moved school's in kindergarten
Me and Karter were friends then
Me and Aiden are friends now
The end.

-Matt

Thankful Couplet

I am grateful for food.
I am grateful for my good mood.

-Lucas

Nature Couplet

Thank you for the trees
and thank you for the bees.

-Hunter

Family Couplet

Thank you for my family
they make me feel happily.

I am thankful for my house.

-Karter

Friends Haiku

I'm thankful for good
school friends like Brooke, Nia, Matt,
Peyton, Levi, Layne.

-Quinn

Health Couplet

My brain wants to play in the rain.
I love my brain.

-Effie

Happy Haiku

I am happy when
I ride dirt bikes and when I
    see Karter, Declan.

-Reed

Thank You Haiku

Thank you for my class.
Thank you for my family.
Thank you for my strength.

-Layne

Thankful Haiku

I am thankful for
my friends, the world, basketball.

-Edward

Family List Poem

I am grateful for
my mom
and my dog
and my dad
and my Karter
and my sun.

-Brooke

My Friends Haiku

My friends are the best.
Friends help each other and care.
    Best friends for ever.

-Kayden

Brothers Haiku

Malix best brother.
I like to play with Archer.
Grateful for brothers.

-Reese

www.ingramcontent.com/pod-product-compliance
Lightning Source LLC
Chambersburg PA
CBHW062112140826
49812CB00058B/1317
9789357449144